ESCAPE ENVY

ESCAPE ENVY

Ace Boggess

Brick Road Poetry Press
www.brickroadpoetrypress.com

Copyright © 2021 by Ace Boggess

Author photo: © 2021 Grace Welch

Cover art: "Nebula and galaxies in space. Abstract cosmos background" © Paul Paladin & "hand opens room door to galaxy" © 4Max (both licensed at stock.adobe.com). Merged image by Keith Badowski from a concept by Ace Boggess.

Library of Congress Control Number: 2021933836
ISBN-13: 978-1-950739-02-8

Published by Brick Road Poetry Press
513 Broadway
Columbus, GA 31902-0751
www.brickroadpoetrypress.com

Brick Road logo by Dwight New

ALL RIGHTS RESERVED
Printed in the United States of America

OTHER BOOKS BY ACE BOGGESS

POETRY
Misadventure
I Have Lost the Art of Dreaming It So
Ultra Deep Field
The Prisoners
The Beautiful Girl Whose Wish Was Not Fulfilled

NOVELS
States of Mercy
A Song Without a Melody

*for Grace
with whom I shared many
of these adventures*

Table of Contents

I.

I Was Heading for Georgia but Saw the Sunrise 3
Traffic Writes Our Biographies 4
My Father's Hearing Aid Broke 5
Bridge 6
As a Passenger in a Golf Cart Searching for Alligators Inside
    a Gated Community 8
Day Trip to the Huntington Museum of Art 9
Rose Garden, Ritter Park 10
Heading into Pittsburgh on the First Day of Summer 11
Hamburger at Hemingway's 12
Crossing 13
At the Art-Walk Noir Exhibit 14
Swans at New Vrindaban 15
More Thoughts after Visiting the Closed-Down West Virginia
    Penitentiary at Moundsville 16
Lunch with the Poet Laureate 17
Two Tickets to Mountain Stage 18
The Kanawha 20
Now That I've Driven South to Visit My Father 21

II.

Escape Envy 25
Assigning a Value 26
The Chaplain's Guitar 27
Candy Man 28
Negative Definition 29
E.R. 31
Hair Dye 32
One Fatality 33
My Condolences 35
Roadwork 36
More Rain 37
Why I Can't Have Superpowers 38
I Met Him Once 39
The Trouble with Existentialism 40

Absent Dearest,..42
Those Nights...43
Facebook Keeps Telling Me..44
Forgive Me, Greatest Foreign Poets..45

III.

Coats..49
Swim..50
Roles..51
Let Me Be Your Dream Dunce...52
Star Star Nothing..53
Information Overload...54
Sing..55
Olivia...56
Rusted Root, 2003..57
Seven Earthlike Planets Found Orbiting Nearby Star...................58
You Salvaged What Was Left of Me...60
Where I Love You..61
It's Raining Glass on Super-Earth..63
I Heard a CNN Commentator Say Generation-Xers Are
   the Adults Now..64
Half-inflated Aluminum Balloon..65
The Moon Reminds Me...67
Why I Can't Draw Portraits..68
Game Seven..69
7 a.m., School Bus Passing..70
Why I Can't Drink My Coffee Black..71
Hard Glare...72
Why I Can't Die Today...73
The End of the Interview...74
Why I Can't Write This Poem..75
There Are Times of Silence..76
The Dream Turned Religious Right Before I Woke..........................77

About the Author...80
Acknowledgments..83

I.

… a land that's fair and bright

I Was Heading for Georgia but Saw the Sunrise

in Virginia the last ten miles or so
as the Interstate dripped down the side
of a high-top at five-percent grade
nothing but view to my left
across the valley I spotted that mountain
shaped like a turtle—shell side & budding neck—
poking its lonely head above a silk line of mist
red & orange set along the fog's plane
like stemless blooms of roses bobbing in a pond
like candles on a silver cake
for those few minutes I had no destination
no hotel room waiting in Columbus
no acquaintances to make
it was as though I stole a pause from life
then froze it without aid of camera's lens
before my car descended past the treeline &
on into North Carolina where
it might as well be raining & it was

Traffic Writes Our Biographies

We are like this, you & I: sitting in a car,
waiting on something to wait for.
Look. Two dragonflies perform their mating dance
in front of our windshield like a movie screen.

We remain the ones not moving.
Our biographies would run long with pages
on which nothing happens,
interspersed with chapters of mayhem.

There's a jumper on the Southside Bridge,
an army of cops trying to talk her down
(which might be the wrong choice of words).
We've paused until it's back to work for you,

or Netflix, more poetry for me,
more silence that speaks loudest in my head.
I've spent so much of my life wanting
the new & unusual, the inspirational

even when it's cruel. I'd like to think
I've answered all the questions. Have I?
Tell me how to move forward.
Tell me how to sing the coming verse.

My Father's Hearing Aid Broke

When I see him, first time in a decade,
at first seeing is all we do: both of us
grayer, fatter, flawed, but smiling
at the lands we've crossed & come to.
If only when he spoke he weren't so loud,
he might not sound like some
hell-singing evangelist,
with me the congregation sleeping,
unwilling to be roused by prophecy,
mystery, shouts. It might be ten more years
before I crawl toward him next,
if both of us live so long &
his promised rapture won't occur,
which, of course, it never does,
not once despite the divinations
of so many fathers just like him.

Bridge

Driving across the Southside Bridge
where iron girders ruffle my radio signal
like a hand through static hair,
I think I might stall traffic,
climb from my Kia, walk to the rail.
Looking down, I'll remember
watching the boats with my father
at Charleston's Sternwheel Regatta.
Speeders ripped water. Colorful
fishing craft trolled near shore.
Partiers on wide, raftlike pontoons
drank their hours, dancing adrift
to harmonies of whatever has-been band
threw noise over stillness.
We sat on the bank, observing,
sometimes pointing like witnesses
to a robber fleeing. I like to believe
my father spoke up then to explain
in *Moby-Dick*-like precision
the clockwork of what we saw,
or maybe to sing along as, say,
The Drifters eased into their choruses.
But he & I were the same in our isolation,
our way of watching without interaction.
We were patients under the dentist's ether:
floating, mesmerized, counting
backward from a random number.
When we regained consciousness,
it would be time to go home,
as I'm doing now: crossing over,
putting a mile behind me:

my car's speakers hiss, whir, clap, sigh, &
I wonder if I've heard this song
or if it's another lie that memory tells.

As a Passenger in a Golf Cart Searching for Alligators Inside a Gated Community

shoeless shanghaied riding the twilight
vehicle jerking beneath me
like a roller coaster on the upslope

what will we do if we see one?
the word 'suddenly' comes to mind
like in a mystery novel a real page-turner

I scan the circumference of the water
hazard—16th hole—then I'm past it
gliding among the prefab houses

palm trees like serifs added to their yards
my stepmother almost seventy
still maneuvers like a hummingbird

she shows me one of the lakes &
another pond a dock a cul-de-sac of reeds
we never locate anything with teeth

before darkness drags us home
"don't give up" she says "they're here &
time to time they come to look for us"

Day Trip to the Huntington Museum of Art

Grace walks by the Renoir without slowing.
I follow, saying, "Renoir," as if I'm a boy
navigating the toy aisle at the supermarket,
begging his mother & father, "I want
the Renoir. Can I have the Renoir,
please, please, please?" She tells me,
"It's not one of his best," but I,
not having seen one up close before,
double back, stand, stare, dazzled &
a bit confused by the red, orange, umber.
It's a blur, alien, so much I find it hard to spot
the *Young Woman in a Landscape*.
I enjoy the painting though,
even the tiny hole that attests to its age &
a handler's careless movement years ago.
It's obvious to me Grace & I won't agree
about the Renoir, although we share a moment
mesmerized by some minor artist's
misty portrait of the moon, then a gallery
filled with newer panoramic visions
of Antarctic ice floes, a few valleys
depicted from a height so intense, precise,
I feel a flash of vertigo as though
I'm standing tiptoed on the edge of a cliff:
this our holy pause to be amazed together
as if sharing a sunset or good news—
what won't happen with the Renoir:
divisive, disputable—which, whether
you like it or not (as together we do),
proves it to be the work of a daring master.

Rose Garden, Ritter Park

Step, step, then circle over imperfect,
treacherous bricks. Flying beetles
like oily blue-green bullets
assail us from all angles
as though thinking us
tender petal-flesh they sought,
still seek after bouncing off &
back to flight. They mistake us
for ax blades of color—
mauve, merlot, & bonfire orange—
though we are pale shadows
in the graveyard of light,
workers sweating through their day
on the perfume assembly line.
We breathe in until we suffocate
from pleasure, when one of us
speaks the safe word, & we go.

Heading into Pittsburgh on the First Day of Summer

Two miles before the Squirrel Hill Tunnel,
I'm stuck in traffic: cars that shudder forward
as if dragged by chains—a few feet,
a few more. On my radio, the forecaster says,

"You're stuck in traffic,"
a dreamlike statement so I feel
the way a carpenter must should he witness
one of his unfinished buildings burn.

I want to start up a conversation
with the news man, tell him,
*Buddy, I already figured that out,
thank you.* He's not listening.

He's moved on to weather,
while I've moved next to not at all.
"Thunderstorm coming," he warns, &
in my rearview, there's the charcoal haze

of violent praising, sky blessing steamy
tarmac, tractor-trailers, hot earth, &
men like me trapped in their boxes,
ever almost there, almost there.

Hamburger at Hemingway's

Not Papa's place strewn with cats,
rifles, maybe (I imagine) whiskey bottles
displayed like a mantelpiece clock
for men who can't tell time.

Just a pub, famously named,
in one gray neighborhood of Pittsburgh.
The young (beardless) man on stage
speaks in riddles & plays a trivia game

with the crowd of students doubling down
on drinks in their happiest hour.
I'm in the next room, eating a burger
that bursts in my mouth like a capsule

spilling its medicine. *Black Angus,*
according to the menu. I take small bites
as if filet mignon, as if kissing
the girl destined to die at the end

of a novel. Could be the best I've eaten
in Pittsburgh. Could be what defines me
as tragic hero, my flaw a hunger,
my appetite an ocean swallowing,

spitting out the gnawed carcass
of the fish. Or else I'm the old man
who caught it, lost it, went to bed starved,
knowing he'll never need sustenance again.

Crossing

the West Virginia/Pennsylvania border
masked in mist
a cataract
turned mother-of-pearl
I know this mile but can't see the sign
coming home invisible the way I always do
like a talented thief
breaking in to his dwelling
where shadows keep watch &
nothing's left to steal

At the Art-Walk Noir Exhibit

Lining the walls of a lawyer's office,
many gritty images: hints of Hitchcock
like the first squirt of hand soap,
though where it lathers mostly falls to shadows,
scenes frozen from the old murder films—
never Sam Spade, but often the mystery woman
who crosses his threshold & smokes a long cigarette.
Grace has a piece like that, first on the left
by the elevator: sultry face ensconced in
negative space—the term she used.
She paints the way I write: hours (days)
of *thinking thinking thinking*,
before hands blink & blaze like beams
at a Pink Floyd laser show.
The best parts are mental anyway,
even for Pollock dripping his candle wax,
bacon grease; even for portraits done by cats
smudging a canvas with their painted paws—
someone had to think of that
just as here in the lawyer's hall,
I'm forced, too, to think of shadows,
those adorning red brick walls,
those in locked steel cabinets
hidden away in files that might read
like cheap detective novels
that end—if they ever do—only
when the bad guy gets away with it.

Swans at New Vrindaban

Cygnets glide across the pond
like replicas of Viking longboats
hand-carved from wood.
On shore, their mother
walks about in the manner of a gorilla:
back straight, head lowered,
wings pounding chest
as she fends off ducks
attempting to steal her feast of seeds.

Swans impress as much as the Palace of Gold,
gardens with flowers I can't name,
stairs leading to ornamented lions,
warm sounds of prayerful chanting,
calls of peacocks like electric crows
plugged into their amplifiers.

They amble with serene hearts
while steeling themselves
for paradise
at the ends of journeys.

More Thoughts after Visiting the Closed-Down West Virginia Penitentiary at Moundsville

Ghosts the guide discusses like memories—
who's to say what's psychic photograph,
what paranormal, spirit orb, ectoplasm, rust?

The dead remember the dead.
The dead hum dirges for themselves,
chant litanies, adding their names to the list.

The state's impenetrable warehouse
now a shrine to retribution—is it haunted
from more than nine hundred murders,

or what claustrophobia we, free guests,
smuggle into ominous lines of cells?
When the façade of brown so Gothic & vast

comes into view, we focus, fail to notice
the looming Native burial mound
across the street—the one for which this town

was named, why no cartographer instead
inked Prisonton, Consburg, or Murderville
on a map along the Highway of Lost Souls.

Lunch with the Poet Laureate

Hardly poetry. I like mine bland,
burned, & free from eccentricities.
Just a slab of charred meat
on toughened bun. What I'm used to:
protest verse for my intestines,
thin mat on a steel slab.

He goes burger also,
prefers juicy,
adding leafy accoutrements on top.

I like the thought of a world in which our gods
grovel with us in the street,
where known & contending
bump their heads on similar doors,
stumble over same chairs,
eat the simple morsels.

A third poet joins us, playing superego
to our friendly duel of ids.
She orders liver
which doesn't belong in sonnets.
I wouldn't wish that on Ashbery,
not even on Billy Collins
who I imagine chooses steak &
spends an hour meditating
on merits of his after-dinner mint.

for Marc Harshman

Two Tickets to Mountain Stage

First act. Opening number.
Already I feel older to hear
the anthem of my generation—
"…entertain us"—slow & soulful,
rendered by a gospel singer,
her maracas chipping away at the air.

This, how I imagine Baby Boomers
must see themselves when they catch a riff
from *Sgt. Pepper's* slanted
into whistling Muzak in the elevator.
Time skipped while they weren't looking,
while I wasn't, lost in some prison

like a penitent pacing his cell
from dawn to whenever. Old,
old, old. Beside me, Grace
hides behind the familiar
grunge-rock words, lets a smile
escape. We've come for Cracker,

that rarity, a band we both enjoy,
but frontmen Lowery & Hickman
have grown older, too:
hair graying, necks rounder
like their guitars.
At least they have fun with it,

while I take all this in,
dancing without leaving
my seat. It's a good night
in which to feel older,

suddenly doddering, ready
for the onset of dementia.

The Kanawha

By the liquor store, the river
has taken on the color of fresh olives
glistening through a martini glass,

plus ice. The parking lot busies
with murky, mud-slapped vehicles.
Patrons amble in & out—pre-

drunk, post-needy—
their expressions reflecting
sickly, pale ash of the atmosphere.

The river though has come alive,
its many whitecapped little feet
dancing a clumsy hoedown with the wind.

Others notice but never stop to watch as I.
Walkers tracing marked paths at the zoo,
they pause by the tiger's cage,

snapping a ghost-fur photograph,
then moving on before the feeding.
What comes next is what is missed,

hardest to witness without standing still.
The river rides its highway
under & past a bridge.

It races itself & erases. It reveals.

Now That I've Driven South to Visit My Father

we talk less as though preparing
for the last distance to come between us

no more ritual of the weekly prison phone call
when all else sounds like sickness

no more *how are you? I'm good
how you holding up?* poor choice

of words *well it's eighty here
so it must be snowing there*

we've finally run out of things to say
we never said enough

unable to agree on politics
religion or what it means to work hard

now he lives on a minor block in a gated community
the size of some cities that have been my home

while I'm clinging to West Virginia
like a sturdy plank from a rent ship &

my cell phone's silence
rings in my ear like tinnitus

I wonder if I should dial his number
just to say *we haven't spoken in a while*

which I'm sure he knows as he knows
that other thing fathers & sons should say

the one that begins in the living room &
ends in another's courtyard far away

II.

… the jails are made of tin

Escape Envy

Dreams that belonged to each of us:
unbroken spirit versus unbreakable walls.
I remember mine as vividly as leg irons:
sniffing pollen from flowers at a highway's edge,
hiding from marshals under a mound
of brittle leaves in the garden,
eating burgers in a dead café. So,
when I heard those two guys made it out
from Clinton Correctional in New York
through a hole in the wall,
along pipes & hidden passageways,
out a manhole into the movie-like rain,
a part of me rejoiced—not the part
that knows human decency,
not the part that wants to be safe
in its discreet new life; no,
that other part that wishes itself bravado,
the visionary weighted down from years of longing.
How it must feel for them to anticipate
a soft mattress, softer arms embracing,
first sniff at sizzle-scents of steak; &
how confusing to learn the world has changed
without them (whatever world they dreamt
of escaping to). It's there I leave them
as though putting down a paperback thriller,
not wanting to read what happens next
when truth does violence to their fantasies,
as it will, & the gray, fermented fruits
of what was believed to be freedom
squeeze sad wine into a glass
from which these men already drank before.

Assigning a Value

Fear equals fear plus
the square root of consequences
divided by time alone.
That's before factoring in
imaginary numbers
for the places you didn't go
when younger, able
to foxtrot & debauch
in unfamiliar cities.
Subtract passport photos
never taken, frequent-
flier miles not acquired.
Reduce further for each night
you didn't speak, the women
you didn't take home
with you, the men.
Then begin your calculus
of woe, figuring self-
worth lost in pills ingested
to rob the equation of fear,
though fear won't leave you &
your obtuse angles.
Fear remains everywhere,
equal now to fear plus
starting over.

The Chaplain's Guitar

The cons never sang like cons in old movies,
a sickly sorrowful melody yearning
for home & girls that brought men low,
a dirge for the lengthy fading,
hymn for mercy from unwelcoming heavens.
A few would rap a line or two &

then move on as if guilty of another crime.
When I felt that familiar soundless emptiness,
with permission I'd go to the education room
where for an hour I could strum chords
on the chaplain's guitar: a relic, an icon,
church of a thousand voices moaning.

Its rusted strings promised me freedom
minutes at a time, hum thrumming
from that holiest hole, although
like all things religious to men like us,
most often it was out of tune &
locked in a cabinet with a single key.

Candy Man

Candy softening scented the cell with cherries,
apples, as if lathered from an herbal shampoo.
The multiple felon, another rough customer,
his hands burned & bruised, rolled balls out of Jolly Ranchers
boiled while snug within the fingers of a stolen latex glove.
Inside each new shell he placed gummy treats: orange slices,
jellybeans. Then he closed the balls & boiled again,
knowing he'd have to work this miracle many times
to turn a minor profit. For the sucker sticks,
he used stripped-down rods of unused cotton swabs,
jamming them in, spear-fishing, careful not to damage
the sweets. Soon, a whole tray finished, the lollipops
sold out among the other hardened men,
the entire cellblock smelling like fruity liquor.
For half an hour, everyone was smiling, free.
Then the maker went back to his task,
overcome by something a man like him
could never admit was love.

Negative Definition

imagine my philosophy prof from 1990,
sophomore year, his crescent-haired lagoon
of scalp, his monotone Eeyore voice

saying *don't think about the President.*
you can't NOT. when you consciously attempt
to conjure a negative, you summon its opposite.

"don't think about the head of state,"
I tell myself. I try, but there he comes
strutting dumbly across my screen

as though I've pulled him from a hat &
now must listen to him jabber
about what a wonderful hat it was &

how he built the best burrow
in a secret pocket in the brim.
"don't think about him," I plead, but

bedazzled brain invites his image on the news
where other loud men draft the chronicle
of lies, arguing over their meanings

as if a crucial line of verse from Frost.
a voice from memory, droning & deliberate,
advises me, *just don't think....*

I cut it off there & put in an effort
as though studying for the blank page
of an exam, but not-thinking doesn't work &

too many others have beaten me to it, &
isn't that the trouble? isn't it? anyway,
didn't my old professor really say,

don't think about polar bears? now
I'm doing that. I'm not thinking about them.
I'm not thinking about them as hard as I can.

E.R.

Arms outstretched, my body now a cock
probing & thrusting through the doughnut eye
of the CT scan. Ho*ld it. Now breathe.*
Hands press like branding irons
against my belly, sides, shoulder blades.
Where does it hurt? Here & here &
a little heavy over there as though a potato.

When I go to the E.R., there are tests to run,
a shot of something. *Fentanyl*, the nurse
says. *It's stronger than morphine.*
What good is the god of sleep
when a mind awakens into pain?

How many times my bed rolls past the gift shop
where stuffed pandas & lions stare at me
through the thin glass like judgmental fools.
How much blood drains out of my arm,
down the saline tube & then back in.

I feel as if in the womb I devoured my twin,
now he shouts, *Let me out,* from my abdomen.

I go through this sham of examination
to have the doctor tell me, *Nothing's wrong*—
a lie—& even drugs I never want
won't offer comfort. I might as well
have been part of the healing ritual
at an old-time revival so the preacher
could swear my faith's not strong enough.

Hair Dye

She bought a box of hair dye,
so I know she didn't kill herself:
the thought kicks up dirt in my head.

It's sort of awful, & I sort of regret it,
but don't know where I might
find coolant for the doubt engine.

She plays hopscotch amongst abysses:
each day a new look at old horrors.
I take her to her visits with the doc,

try to keep her occupied, &
I feel like a ghost in the garden.
I latch onto whatever sounds like hope, &

what's more hopeful than hair dye?
Brown Six-A, I think: closer to her natural
than the various shades of low

self-esteem she's worn for months.
Better a dye job than a die job: another
unpleasant thought. So's *do-it-yourself*—

a phrase I'm glad is missing from the box
as if a sign inside a casket that avers,
If you can read this, you're too close.

One Fatality

What a day, she must have thought,
for travel—steaming ninety, sun-
stroked, stoked—before clouds
approached like battleships
waggling their mean guns.
How long did it take her to understand
she was roving from a point in space
to nowhere? That the end arrived
in advance of the end intended?

TV news flashed pictures
of her candy-apple compact car
upside-down on fire. In stills,
we could almost see passersby
staring through their dotted windows.
Who doesn't love to witness
someone else's catastrophic failure?
How we stared at the screen

for O.J. Simpson's slow-
speed Bronco chase.
How amazed we were by those
seven comet fragments
slamming into Jupiter—
elsewhere, far from touching us.
No one wants a friend to overdose,
lover to acquire cancer. But,

one orange-red eruption in Hawaii
looks so vivid from a living room
in West Virginia. Pawns
must be sacrificed to the glory

of our eyes. Some drive
to their deaths, some on a highway
near my house. What hand pushing
the next piece knows regret?

My Condolences

I'm sorry for your loss. I'm sorry for your loss.
I must practice lest I get words wrong:
this simple thing I don't know how to say.

I've never been a mourner, never worn
those black glasses grief prescribes.

I confess that I can't empathize
with what way you react when people die—
now someone close, your heart, your wife.

How might I sneak you past
the weepers in this sadness study group,
I who've not yet read the introduction
to their text? *I'm sorry for your loss,*

I'll tell you, mechanical as a grinding clock,
but why should you listen? What good
will it do? I'd be like a pallbearer
showing up with broken arms—

more dead weight on the uneven path,
drunken lout who came too late,
singing his song of *sorry for your loss.*

Roadwork

I once thought I'd die in traffic amidst shattered spines
of cars, or by infarction—one hand white-
knuckled on the wheel, the other raising a fist
to no one close enough to smell the sweat of my anger.
Not today as five minutes turns into an hour.
I sit calmly, blowing smoke, counting cones
lined up like convicts in their orange jumpers,
or staring into the empty squad car on the shoulder
blazing its sulfurous candles, a scarecrow in a concrete field.
I watch the crew taking a break for sandwiches & coffee
while I crawl here on my belly. I wonder why
I ever felt the need to rush (the movie restarts later &
the grocer's doors stay unlocked forever).
In those days I made a sundial of the gearshift
as though I could measure my remaining breaths
in the space between Drive One & Three.

More Rain

Silver dress in a dark room,
bodiless beneath its shimmering.
The dance won't cease:
hour after hour dampening
severed necks of cut grass,
concrete steps leading from the patio,
the newspaper in its flimsy
bathing suit—plastic, indecent.
How I wanted this, & want it
to end like a miracle
having gone on too long,
humbling the sacred at first &
then ho-humming.

Why I Can't Have Superpowers

I don't feel villainous
until lasers clack like pool balls from my eyes,
hands devolve into vicious claws:
get out of my way.
I look back at fantasies from childhood &
watch them turn, think,
So, I'm the bad guy here?

I separate atoms of vehicle & driver
in front of me on a slow day of stern, serious
traffic lights. I melt vault doors
using my flamethrower arms.
Mind control? Don't ask.
Really, don't. Plato: the invisible man
makes himself king—who could stop him?

Here I come with my narcotic breath,
my army of others like me,
eager to strap you to the gurney,
teach you sleep in bleak transcendence,
let you learn to love suffering
until we beg for mercy from ourselves:
Oh, great & horrible brute, what have I done?

I Met Him Once

He seemed reserved, inward,
too calm for the cloak
of frenzy his reputation wore.

He drank little, said less—
no harsh words for poets
we were there to judge.

His best friend Kinder
downed a fifth of Jack &
never made an appearance.

That's more what I expected
from a celebrated author,
a reviled one—

because his novel *Crum*
tore at the carcass
of a place, chewed its guts,

then spit them on the ground.
I remember him milder—
beard sculpted, hair precise—

although his eyes kept pistols
loaded & quill already
caked with ink.

He swore he could handle
either, take you down
one way or the other.

in memory of Lee Maynard

The Trouble with Existentialism

You don't exactly pick up
a copy of *Being & Nothingness* &,
there on page 645, find Sartre

discoursing on one's being-for-orchids,
one's being-toward-riverbanks-at-sunset.
You can't go searching through pages

of Nietzsche's *Will to Power*,
hoping to catch sentimental Friedrich mid-
aphorism, stating: "Man surrenders gladly

for a gentle kiss." It's all struggling for control,
to survive, to find oneself or freedom in despair,
struggling for the privilege to struggle more.

Sure, there's Camus with his man-is-defined-
by-his-make-believe, but a single
tragic-sense-of-life keeps that in line.

Yet I want to assure you you might traverse
the land of Kierkegaard without contracting
sickness unto death, fear & trembling,

either/or. Know only that
townsfolk you meet won't press
fingers into the pit of your back,

stroke your inner thigh.
They are not at all like you
with your being-for-flush-of-skin,

sighing at night with will to embrace.
Even in love & sleep they lack your
being-toward-poems-by-moonlight.

Absent Dearest,

I walked among the graves alone
except for those dead names
collected in the whisper-basket of my tongue.
Crossing muddy easements, my face slicked with fine rain
that brought cologne's scent like wine & citrus off my skin,
I knew no one's *Lithia Ledford, wife of Lee;*
no *Sherry, Raymond, Eric & Baby Qualls;*
not a single *Irvin Bell, infant son of Erma Jean.*
I met them, faded images enshrined in frames:
*Lewis Benson, Elsey Lamar, James Everett Eudy
the third, the fourth & the fifth.*
Were you there to witness their Civil War memorials,
their fragile elephants carved like marble teddy bears,
to count their dates & read their names aloud with me—
Mrs. Lazano, Hope Running, Rev. Ronald Lovinggood—
you would have welcomed love into your breath.
Distant, your name waited in twilit West Virginia,
surrounded by graves for rivers, shifting plates
that have no names we know, their monuments
extending to the clouds. Still, I praised your name,
Love, strolling through the cemetery dark.
It was the voice of reason in my head,
the voice of remembering
as though I held your hand & led you
from that silence, voiceless absence
of your name, my name, their whispers.

Those Nights

night of colors & night of sound   blues & blue notes
sweat slinging with sex-mad zeal off Roy's *Takamin*e strings
a festive bar's passion room & you with spirit
blunted   obsessing about balloons
your method to forget the fight that finished a friendship
while I forgave the music for its happiness &
did my best to help you locate yours   O & one
night we spent in an Ashland graveyard hiding from police
you & I like lovers needing neither word nor touch
you there to see your monument that weeps
I for a comet that never came   clouds too thick
sky burned by searchlights   so many nights
we bundled our sufferings in a canvas sack &
drowned them in the river like a bottled message
pleading for help but left unsigned   too many nights
restless & not   urgent & not   waiting for a happening
this night answers those   a compendium
tonight we await our emptying music
until these distant beds in which we never sleep
might seem less crowded by those nights   nights
we loved & did not love ourselves

Facebook Keeps Telling Me

I should be friends with my ex-wife,
extend handshake & chivalrous salute,
as if we might hang out
somewhere between servers &
play Gin Rummy, digital checkers,
as if not-enemies isn't enough;
we have to like each other, &
our posts. Her face appears,
sadly smiling, on my screen
like a phantom, like any
of one hundred thousand memories,
ambiguous. + Add Friend,
the social network strong-arms me,
demanding I send a new request
as though she wouldn't request in turn
twenty years of her life back, &
I wouldn't find it too disturbing
to read about her relationship status,
thumb through pictures of her travels
to beaches, zoos, concerts, cathedrals,
with whomever might prove
martyr enough for love.
I'm much too busy regretting,
also trying to forget, & dancing
in a dark & empty room,
while wondering how I should
pitch Facebook on an + Add
Not-Enemy button for those
we'd rather not know, except we do.

Forgive Me, Greatest Foreign Poets

That I do not know the weight & pressure
of rifle's stock against a skull,
that I have not seen tanks
roll in from the east like snapping turtles
with their mean, murky shells.
I am no hollow of a tree
in which men hide the bones of their dead.
I haven't tasted my own teeth
on my tongue's root. Nor
have I chosen which fingers to keep &
lose. I apologize to you,
greatest foreign poets
who have been trampled by horses,
forced to employ the labor of your hands
or orifices, if I presume
my darkrooms are as filled with negatives
as yours. I can take a punch,
describe for you the inside of a jail cell
dissimilar to the ones you despise.
I know what my blood looks like
when I cup it in my palm. Yet,
I'm sorry, greatest foreign poets,
that I am such an infant
crawling along with your unrelenting march.
Pardon me if I stop to suck a finger
while I study the lines you've drawn
with heavy boot prints in the painted mud.

III.

… a lake of stew and of whiskey too

Coats

Grace swears nobody in Hawaii sold coats.
"Who would need one?" she says.
She moved to West Virginia as a child, &
her first winter: two feet of snow,
emptiness, panoramic photonegative
of some burn-scarred Baptist hell.
Then, cold: Zen & the art of freezing to death.
Sunshine leached out of her skin
in a state where even the homeless had leather,
wool- & fur-trimmed, trench, faux fox,
the Russian Great-, handmade parkas
stitched with nails & old, discarded quilts.
She wanted to flee. "This has never
been my home," she tells me,
decades not enough to spark &
warm her wintry body—scarf
to match: emerald, flowered, silk.

Swim

Put aside the suicides, the sore throat, bad heart,
complaints probing your left ear & your right.

Sink into denser space,
matter mattering in its easing.

Your arms beat away the foul-mouthed politicking.
They slash through plasma screens set to CNN

on which nitwits are preening. There:
stroke, release. All that kicking batters rage

you don't want to experience.
Run in the water. Walk on it. Glide.

Stillness you feel fills consciousness
with cotton candy. Holes drilled into your skull

by one death or another
will be patched with mud, bleached bright.

You found the tunnel, lifejacket, parachute.
You land, move, climb the ladder, &

as you reclaim your heaviness,
your heaviness is what you leave behind.

Roles

It was late, & you were
wearing your widow suit,
black of 1870s chic,
loaded with bustle.
I did my best Doc
Holliday—Val's version, cock-
sure & half-goofy. You
laughed. I laughed. Val
would've laughed if he were here
watching me paw at your corset,
pull the strings to tighten it.
Moments like this,
we feel happiest,
field mice exploring
magnificent catacombs
of a dusty closet.
I act out in otherness;
you dress up the same:
not faces of whatever
force invented us,
but what we make
of ourselves
when we're at play.

Let Me Be Your Dream Dunce

Bright-eyed desperado on a mission for disaster.

Snow-cap climber heading for the peak
      of Mt. Oh-no-one-goes-there-ever.

View-taker who topples over the railing of the boat
      into choppy waters you barely save me from.

Let me let go of rope, map, & stars—

I'll walk into danger as a fawn
      not fast enough to flee the mountain lion,

tell you philosophies of nothing while we sit
      in your dream-Jacuzzi in our clothes.

Let me be clumsy, cuss, rant, & stub my toe
      on a jag in the earth,
      my forehead once more on the jeweled moon.

Star Star Nothing

fluke of solar trickery tickling Earth's axial autumn angle
according to the local news *aurora borealis*
might dazzle this far south tonight
but when I go outside I see no emerald flickers
massaging the scalp of the world with fizzy bright shampoo
just black space star star nothing
a hint of haze set off by city glow
never have I witnessed the billowing cape
jade mask or bold abyss gazing back
as if *this far south* is north of here
reminder how empty the universe seems &
in it that I exist at all must be improbable
myth one atom tells the next as each looks up
but never quite makes out my greenish eyes

Information Overload

The doctor says, "Her heart is good:
all of it, here & here & here,"
pointing to quartered photo
showing pictures from four angles.
I don't laugh, though I find it funny
that when you declare someone has a good heart,
you then have to be specific,
like when a meteorologist on the evening news
announces storms rolling through,
then points behind at the green screen
with its digital map that only we can see,
says, like a surgeon, "Here & here & here."
It's not enough to know there will be light-
ning at first, followed by darkness
when the power fails. We require
intimate details of a celebrity's sex life,
General's scandals, Senator's funeral Mass.
I thank the doctor & accept his glossy
as if he's an aspiring actor seeking a role,
then go back to the waiting room to wait
like an obsessive-compulsive
counting steps of the minute hand,
the freckles & lines on every stranger's face.

Sing

My mother swears I told her
she could hold me
but not sing,
when I was still unbroken by the world.

Would I rob anyone of music?
Demand silence from a voice
desperate with melodies,
hummed lines—high-pitched, overcoming?

Maybe I fell too near to sleep
or hadn't learned to feel
emotional notes.

Did I want to change the station,
seeking upbeat riffs less sad, gospel Elvis?

That must have been the 70s, &
I a blunt object, as children are.

Today, I want to say, *Sing, Mother.*
Never mind the critic,
miser of hymns.
Sing like you never witnessed deaths.
Sing like years have shown you far too many.

Olivia

Grace asked me about my first crush, &
I had to think, really strain to find Olivia
Newton-John—the version of her from *Xanadu*,
a big-haired disco muse on roller skates.
I was just a kid & didn't know anything
about sex, or anything about anything
except that she beamed like starlight in her tight,
white pants, & of course she danced.
Her face sanded down to polished smooth,
her Australian accent, how she sang—
always to her lover in films—
were what I hoped for: a woman who'd sing to me,
voice an erotic candle flickering, oh, the melody,
upbeat mostly. I had forgotten. Sure,
years pass, & a child who dreams
becomes a man with visions, some of ugliness,
many with hurt, where even songs
he hears in his head are copies
of older songs, their basslines muted,
drums slowed, guitars mourning
the loss of their first love.

Rusted Root, 2003

Day of the Northeast Outage when the grid went down.
I carried my concert ticket & handful of pills
on a three-hour drive to Louisville,
chain-smoked cloves, listened to AM radio
for news: how far did darkness reach?

I didn't concern myself if there were looting, riots,
cannibal hordes roaming the wasteland of old America.

Just the music & whether I'd hear it.

This day seemed some shell game conning tourists,
whereas I was desperate to touch sound,
remember how a melody feels to skin.

I doubted I'd be lucky, find Kentucky lit up
as with tracer rounds adorning the skies over Baghdad
when other nearby states were sans serif,
burnt out, bland, black as lack of music

in a man's heart. I cursed the road I crossed,
arrived to discover the power on,
doors opened, performers in back preparing &
unaware of nearness to the absence of a song.

Seven Earthlike Planets Found Orbiting Nearby Star

Footpath of the universe,
street to door,
dwarf to empty
extrasolar cosmos.

Maybe water, mud,
or char. Better
change our vacation plans
for the next millennium.

Forty light years—
not so far
we can't dream it
like a trip cross-

country to Seattle
though we don't yet
own a car.
Such sights to see.

Might be strange
new dinosaurs,
colorful shimmering
lights in the sky:

aurora something-
else-alis.
With proximity &
perception, we envision

vacuum rides
through folded-space

pneumatic tubes
to get there,

away from here at least,
until the situation settles,
as if we could ever
be far enough from home.

You Salvaged What Was Left of Me

The year I stopped caring if a hood would cover me,
I'd been fired from my newspaper job in Martinsburg &
now worked beside you in the record store/
head shop/ sex room where business suits
meant jeans & tie-dyes or concert tees.
Stuck living with my parents, I smoked weed daily &
drank or popped whatever I laid hands on
as I waited hour after hour for the world to end.
It got so bad I started reading Sartre for fun.
Yet there you were, looking up at me with eyes like martini olives,
hair black & blond, roping bangs like forelegs of a tarantula.
You smiled, sniffing at me like a cocker spaniel.
You made demands, telling me what you wanted
as if any of it mattered, as if I did.
We lay together on your mattress on the floor,
listening to Syd Barrett & breathing in
coconut smoke off incense cones.
I wanted to tell you then how you rescued me,
forced me to stop, drop & roll to put out a fire.
Call it laziness or cowardice. Call it insanity,
call it youth—I left the gratitude language unspoken.
Is it too late to say I embrace you & the memory of you
such that even recollections of my own self-
doubt & misery show their faces in warmly blushing hues?
I haven't let go despite years like miles between us,
so you save me again & again *ad infinitum*
like the greatest play in a ballgame shown &
reshown on TV long after it's old news &
I'm the only viewer left who wants to see.

Where I Love You

Numb to night in the passenger seat
of a black Ford Tempo,
with a pinstripe passion red,
on the long road to Calamity Café.

In a record store fumbling among incense packs &
tee shirts swirling with faces of the dead:
John, Jimi, Jerry—our names don't begin with J,
so we'll never be famous, never die.

In a faux-Italian restaurant
drinking instant cappuccino from our mugs
while we wait for the pills to kick in.

Then, near Columbus,
where Lux in vinyl sings your heart to misery,
back to bruises, breath to desire. Also,

in the hospital's waiting room,
the two of us holding hands
while we compare the faces of our friends
to animals: this one a lion, that a tired hound.

In your apartment with its
mattress on the floor like a funeral barge,
surrounded by candles &
cats you put out before talking lust.

In the darkness to follow: what always follows.

In taverns & prisons.

In theaters where we watch the latest alien invasion
action-packed thrilling comedy romance
for those hours of escape
although escape is never what we want.

It's Raining Glass on Super-Earth

Couldn't we go there to see it
for a couple hours in a bubble
more protective than one
we spend fragile lives inside?

I promise to be caring, pay attention,
hold your hand, kiss you
under penumbral refractions
from its one or many moons.

We will witness a tickertape parade
with violence,
glitter, blunt-force trauma to the land.

We want this, you & I:
to go elsewhere, see
something messy & raw as a broken egg.

I will love you while it burns, brightens,
shimmers, & sparks in silicate spasms.

Please, yes, let it smash its windows,
mirrors, leaving us blind
to ourselves, the whole shebang.

I Heard a CNN Commentator Say Generation-Xers Are the Adults Now

I want a new reality show called
The Boring Sex Lives of Middle-aged Men.

I want to hear strangers discussing
side effects of pills used as directed.

There's entertainment in simple things:
headaches, hiccoughs, parallel parking,

Walmart shopping at 3 a.m.
I want a look inside the cubicle.

Give me the ho-hum, humdrum
revival tent at the slacker festival;

a museum of living-room couches,
one with a parents'-basement wing.

It's all so goddamned interesting.
I feel like a three-legged rhino

running to leap a thirty-foot ravine:
clumsy, bizarre & Sisyphean.

This is my outcry & urgent scream.
I want again to be young enough not to care.

Half-inflated Aluminum Balloon

skips drunkenly
at the shoulder
a directionless toad
a pup bounding
toward birds
in the tallest tree
it can't get lift
despite a fine diet
of helium wind
snowflakes barely
heavier than nothing
painted on each side

in grade school we
loosed the full ones
for an experiment
a flock of them
a gaggle
a murder
sent them *en masse*
with messages
hello mostly
my name is…
no one wrote back
the sky is a wide sea
for little bottles

I like to think some kids
wrote *help me*
Scott loves Beverly
or *if train X*

leaves Philadelphia...
I imagine notes
fluttering down
like burning leaves
escaping a fire
their vessels
deflated
hopeless

there's no message
from the 1970s here
just a knight errant
on its erratic quest
its heart isn't in it
as it searches
for a place to settle
itself among the weeds

The Moon Reminds Me

like a string tied around the finger of the Earth
that whatever I might have forgotten
continues

waiting for me to notice
to ease into morning
6 a.m.

I step outside to collect the paper &
my thoughts
then suddenly (as in a mystery

when the detective finds a scrap from a letter
in the fireplace—
one burnt brilliant clue)

I'm staring at that bright penumbral halo
igniting clouds at the near horizon
the full moon

resembling a lemon-pudding pie
strewn with holiday lights
invites me to eat up

take notes on how it never leaves me hungry
even in the loneliest hours
between sleep & dawn

Why I Can't Draw Portraits

I suck at stick figures: they lean & sag
like fuzzy old couples hiding out in their summer homes.

I never saw myself sketching trees, saying, *Breathe,
breathe*, while I faked the leaves.

Those pictures of rabbits in backs of comic books?
The ones with captions like *Are you an Artist?*

I couldn't trace them to their warrens.
Turtles, too, eluded me. Their lines

ran faster than my pen. During school years,
I managed a pretty mushroom cloud, &

I think I depicted the soda can, not quite fizzing.
During my stay in rehab, I painted a likeness of my right hand,

palm up, cupping blood that was also mine,
nightmarish vision I survived—as close as I've come

to anything human: face with a story &
mouth with which to tell it, eyes reflected back at me

as if from darkness of undergrowth
that could topple a man afraid to call for help.

Game Seven

I dreamt about hockey & zombies.
Not together, but part of a sequence of events
my subconscious gave like alms. First,
monsters: grotesque images straight from AMC,
sleepy-eyed, yawning their breath like rust &
onions. I think I ran away. Next thing,
I'm standing front row by the Plexiglas,
shouting "Motherfucker!" at a player on the ice.
Not one of Tampa's goons the Penguins
duel tonight—game seven, conference finals,
for a chance to compete for the Stanley Cup.
Nameless skater thugs with bristly playoff beards &
meanness. Easy for me to make that connection
between last night's vision & tonight's violent action.
Mind? Id? Freud? Sure, but what about
the ghouls? Do they mean hockey,
too? How they'd slide across the surface,
limbs flailing like in old cartoons.
I'd like to see them wearing Tampa jerseys,
hip-checked hard against the boards,
splattered—Pittsburgh scores at will,
the tension gone.

7 a.m., School Bus Passing

Its taillights distant airplanes
slicing through the mist of chilled November drizzle.
It doesn't stop. No children left—all grown,
moved away. Or else, the pick-up point's
been gerrymandered out of existence,
bringing silence where before those darkened houses
refused to hold their tongues,
spouting playfulness each morning,
sounds of laughter equal to or greater than
the sounds of rain like steam hiss &
finger snap. Everything changes: I,
those kids, the school-bus driver,
even the English language,
providing new ways to curse & regret
what I should've noticed sooner
were I not always hiding out
in a room with no windows &
more imagination than good sense.

Why I Can't Drink My Coffee Black

Bitter, lonely pool at night—
too much it reminds me of prison
like a tar pit filled with dinosaur bones.

How I once stared into it—instant,
water microwaved or lukewarm from the tap—&
saw my reflection, malformed in its murky mirror.

The penitentiary was half-&-halfless,
lifeless, bland despite its fires.
Its black coffee clamped new shackles

on the extra limbs inside me,
invisible to me, although I felt them tugging,
strained against their chains.

The commissary lady experimented once
with selling jugs of powdered creamer, &
for a few months, my heart

paroled, until someone in administration
figured out the fine grains
might be used to build a bomb

(the science of flashpoint). Then,
again: black water. I learned to swim
there in the isolation of my sadness,

a caught thief banished from Xanadu,
its warmest liquors & delicious, bliss-
inducing, non-dairy milk of paradise.

Hard Glare

The pickup blazing its halogen brights
like two spotlighting helicopters
speeds into the cul-de-sac,
truck's high beams a midnight sunrise
through a grid of blinds
before the driver realizes his mistake,
backs up to leave, carrying daytime
with him like lightning in a Tesla coil.
Who needs to witness so much at once
while noticing so little? Who
disturbs the peace without a sound?
I'd go outside & shake my fist at him
as if taunting an invisible god in the sky,
all-seeing, but he's gone now,
pulling away amidst meteor streaks
of taillights ascending, night-bold,
stars red giants that grant no wishes,
proof, I think, the bastard's *lucky,* too.

Why I Can't Die Today

I'd rather be turned into an oak or walk brush-
stroked like a smudged thumbprint
into a painting—"Starry Night,"
"The Scream"—but it's the cardboard box
for me, flushed toilet,
my name scratched on a rock.
I'll keep going as long as words do,
because cigarettes kill slowly,
consciousness rides soundwaves, &
there's much left I haven't seen.
All I wanted was to play a few songs
in front of someone who would love me once.
I've done that twice. Now I'm searching
for undiscovered colors—I can name them,
leave my mark in the lipstick aisle.
Maybe then I'll see a physician
who can tell me how short life is &
how much time I have to waste.
I might seek out a famous Picasso,
press my face to its canvas & lean in,
dragging behind me my red guitar
to jam along in concert with his blue.

The End of the Interview

You had your office: a light in shadow,
of the shadow & wearing it;
behind you a window dull as a wall;
in front, a desk between us.
Your eyes chewed at the meat of me
as your left hand pressed the red button
on a microcassette recorder. Then,
I awoke to the sound of my alarm
whirring gently as a loud wind &
asking nothing the same as you,
robbed of your first question
as though morning were a thief
demanding just the topmost bill in your purse.
So, I ask you, what was the purpose
of the interview? To expose me?
Make me famous? Set the record straight?
You wanted a story—*the* story—
I never got my chance to tell about the prison
I built for myself with steel & brilliant colors;
about rivers I walked beside those nights
I was almost alone & not alone;
about my new book which has monsters
in it, all of whom look like me.
You wanted answers. I gave none,
but will open up should you
put down your reporter's pen &
contact me again in the noisy,
unnatural space in which we live.

Why I Can't Write This Poem

I'm an underqualified overachiever
with slack green eyes &
frizzy, swirling flagellates for hair.
I don't fit the profile except in mugshots
where I make an attractive silhouette.

I think about too many things & miss my cue,
busy wondering what race cars look like
in the Andromeda galaxy.

Often, I'm afraid
of the sound my voice makes when it cracks
the empty, quiet spine of my room.

My socks hate me.
My sweats cling like a wide-eyed ex.
This pen? It doesn't need me, so I let it rest.

Yesterday I was watching a movie about Mars
when I should've been here, hunched over,
guarding my words like prison chow.

This page looks up to me like I'm its father,
but as with fathers,
the infallible illusion fades
after all the times I'm proven wrong.

There Are Times of Silence

when my head whirs & clatters like a dusty fan.
I can't close the browser window in my brain
long enough to enjoy a blank screen,
ease into an afternoon of rest.

I should be doing X, I think. *She said Y, but why?* I think.
*The government is, the country is, the ignorance of men,
my own. I'm a failure & a god,* I think,
ideas passing in contrails rather than lasting comets' tails.

Talk to myself, although it's not me to whom I speak,
but those I know: my head full of full conversations
we won't have in dim bars or crowded halls
innocuously passing. Sometimes songs erupt inside:

dormant volcanoes believed extinct. I don't wish
to sing along, so listen as if to a stereo through the wall.
I can't mute it, can't make out words I once memorized
in ghost-gray off-key melodies like these.

The Dream Turned Religious Right Before I Woke

all I remember though earlier it found an action plot
the what I've lost as surely as the why
it shifted into prayer—not mine
not my beliefs but some
I wasn't offended bothered angry
but spotted with easiness
as though I wore heating pads
over aches & wounds
as though all gathered in this group & I
were prisoners to the same Grendel-hearted warden
our deaths would follow or maybe escape
should the dream not break when it did
leaving me untroubled as a gray squirrel at rest
warmed on its branch by the sun

About the Author

Ace Boggess is author of six books of poetry, including *The Prisoners*, *Ultra Deep Field*, and *I Have Lost the Art of Dreaming It So*, as well as the novels *States of Mercy* and *A Song Without a Melody*. He earned his B.A. from Marshall University and his J.D. from West Virginia University. He serves as Senior Editor at *The Adirondack Review* and Associate Editor at *The Evening Street Review*. His poems have appeared in *Michigan Quarterly Review*, *Harvard Review*, *Notre Dame Review*, *J Journal*, *North Dakota Quarterly*, and many other journals. His awards include the Robert Bausch Fiction Award and a fellowship from the West Virginia Commission on the Arts. In addition, he was locked up for five years in the West Virginia prison system, an experience which has been the basis for much of his writing. He currently resides in Charleston, West Virginia.

Acknowledgments

The author wishes to thank the following publications in which these poems first appeared, sometimes in slightly different forms:

Alexandria Quarterly: "Why I Can't Have Superpowers"
Anti-Heroin Chic: "Hair Dye"
Aquifer: The Florida Review Online: "Roles" and "Let Me Be Your Dream Dunce"
Atlanta Review: "You Salvaged What Was Left of Me" and "The Trouble with Existentialism"
Bluestem: "Coats"
Borderlands: Texas Poetry Review: "Candy Man"
Burnt Pine Magazine: "Those Nights"
The Chattahoochee Review: "I Was Heading for Georgia but Saw the Sunrise" and "Forgive Me, Greatest Foreign Poets"
Chiron Review: "Olivia"
Coe Review: "Lunch with the Poet Laureate"
The Cortland Review: "The Dream Turned Religious Right Before I Woke"
cream city review: "The Chaplain's Guitar"
Eunoia Review: "Roadwork"
Exposition Review: "At the Art-Walk Noir Exhibit"
The Fourth River: "Hamburger at Hemingway's"
Gamut: "Heading into Pittsburgh on the First Day of Summer"
Glass: "My Condolences"
The Hamilton Stone Review: "Rusted Root, 2003"
Hawai'i Pacific Review: "I Met Him Once"
Hobo Camp Review: "Crossing"
The Indianapolis Review: "Bridge"
Love's Executive Order: "Negative Definition"
Maryland Literary Review: "Assigning a Value"

Mason Street: "Swans at New Vrindaban"
The Meadow: "Where I Love You"
Mojave River Review: "Why I Can't Die Today"
Mud Season Review: "E.R."
the museum of americana: "One Fatality"
Naugatuck River Review: "Day Trip to the Huntington Museum of Art"
Noble / Gas Qtrly: "Hard Glare" and "Star Star Nothing"
Open: a Journal of Arts & Letters: "I Heard a CNN Commentator Say Generation-Xers Are the Adults Now"
The Peacock Journal: "More Rain"
The Pedestal Magazine: "Why I Can't Draw Portraits"
The Pikeville Review: "The Kanawha"
Pittsburgh Poetry Review: "7 a.m., School Bus Passing"
Poetry East: "The End of the Interview"
Pomona Valley Review: "It's Raining Glass on Super-Earth"
Rattle: "Escape Envy," "Facebook Keeps Telling Me" and "Absent Dearest,"
Red River Review: "Two Tickets to Mountain Stage"
River Styx: "Now That I've Driven South to Visit My Father" and "Why I Can't Drink My Coffee Black"
San Antonio Review: "There Are Times of Silence"
Sierra Nevada Review: "Game Seven"
Slipstream: "The Moon Reminds Me"
The South Carolina Review: "Half-Inflated Aluminum Balloon"
Tar River Poetry: "Swim"
Tinderbox Poetry Journal: "As a Passenger in a Golf Cart Searching for Alligators Inside a Gated Community"
West Texas Literary Review: "More Thoughts after Visiting the Closed-Down West Virginia Penitentiary at Moundsville"

Whale Road Review: "My Father's Hearing Aid Broke"
The William and Mary Review: "Traffic Writes Our Biographies"
The Worcester Review: "Information Overload"
Xavier Review: "Why I Can't Write This Poem"

Thanks to *Mud Season Review* for nominating "E.R." for Best of the Net, and to *Slipstream* for nominating "The Moon Reminds Me" for the Pushcart Prize.

The section titles are from "Big Rock Candy Mountain" by Harry McClintock.

Our Mission

BRICK ROAD POETRY PRESS

The mission of Brick Road Poetry Press is to publish and promote poetry that entertains, amuses, edifies, and surprises a wide audience of appreciative readers. We are not qualified to judge who deserves to be published, so we concentrate on publishing what we enjoy. Our preference is for poetry geared toward dramatizing the human experience in language rich with sensory image and metaphor, recognizing that poetry can be, at one and the same time, both familiar as the perspiration of daily labor and as outrageous as a carnival sideshow.

Available from Brick Road Poetry Press

www.brickroadpoetrypress.com

The Word in Edgewise by Sean M. Conrey

Household Inventory by Connie Jordan Green

Practice by Richard M. Berlin

A Meal Like That by Albert Garcia

Cracker Sonnets by Amy Wright

Things Seen by Joseph Stanton

Battle Sleep by Shannon Tate Jonas

Lauren Bacall Shares a Limousine by Susan J. Erickson

Ambushing Water by Danielle Hanson

Having and Keeping by David Watts

Assisted Living by Erin Murphy

Credo by Steve McDonald

The Deer's Bandanna by David Oates

Creation Story by Steven Owen Shields

Touring the Shadow Factory by Gary Stein

American Mythology by Raphael Kosek

Waxing the Dents by Daniel Edward Moore

Speaking Parts by Beth Ruscio

Also Available from Brick Road Poetry Press

www.brickroadpoetrypress.com

Dancing on the Rim by Clela Reed

Possible Crocodiles by Barry Marks

Pain Diary by Joseph D. Reich

Otherness by M. Ayodele Heath

Drunken Robins by David Oates

Damnatio Memoriae by Michael Meyerhofer

Lotus Buffet by Rupert Fike

The Melancholy MBA by Richard Donnelly

Two-Star General by Grey Held

Chosen by Toni Thomas

Etch and Blur by Jamie Thomas

Water-Rites by Ann E. Michael

Bad Behavior by Michael Steffen

Tracing the Lines by Susanna Lang

Rising to the Rim by Carol Tyx

Treading Water with God by Veronica Badowski

Rich Man's Son by Ron Self

Just Drive by Robert Cooperman

The Alp at the End of My Street by Gary Leising

About the Prize

BRICK ROAD POETRY PRESS

The Brick Road Poetry Prize, established in 2010, is awarded annually for the best book-length poetry manuscript. Entries are accepted August 1st through November 1st. The winner receives $1000 and publication. For details on our preferences and the complete submission guidelines, please visit our website at www.brickroadpoetrypress.com.

Winners of the Brick Road Poetry Prize

2019

Return of the Naked Man by Robert Tremmel

2018

Speaking Parts by Beth Ruscio

2017

Touring the Shadow Factory by Gary Stein

2016

Assisted Living by Erin Murphy

2015

Lauren Bacall Shares a Limousine by Susan J. Erickson

2014

Battle Sleep by Shannon Tate Jonas

2013

Household Inventory by Connie Jordan Green

2012

The Alp at the End of My Street by Gary Leising

2011

Bad Behavior by Michael Steffen

2010

Damnatio Memoriae by Michael Meyerhofer

CPSIA information can be obtained
at www.ICGtesting.com
Printed in the USA
LVHW110253180521
687666LV00008B/487

9 781950 739028